William and the WIND
The Story of WILLIAM KAMKWAMBA

Written by Shannen Yauger

Illustrated by Bojana Stojanovic

CHAPTER 1
Hunger

The hot Malawi sun beat
down on the empty fields and
a small grove of mango trees.
There was a swift wind, and
the three boys under the trees
were happy for the breeze,
even if it was a warm one.

"Wow, is it ever hot!" William said to his cousin Geoffrey and his friend Gilbert. The boys rested in the heat of the day. The shade of the mango tree did very little to help them stay cool.

"It is always hot," said Geoffrey sadly.

"I am hungry," said Gilbert, looking longingly at the empty fields around them.

William wiped sweat from his face and looked around his family's farm. He used to be able to see so much maize, which is a kind of sweet corn.

The maize was very important to William's family. It was used not only for their food but also to make them money.

But when fourteen-year-old William looked out now, the farm looked very different. Months before, heavy rains had washed away most of the newly sprouted plants, and only a bit of maize was left. After the rain stopped, it never started again. Now it had not rained in a very long time, and most of the plants left in the fields had dried up and died,

not just in his father's fields, but in all of William's country.

"I am hungry too, friend," William said to Gilbert. "I am always hungry now. We all are."

William's family, like many others, was very hungry. Without maize, no one had enough food to eat. Since maize was made into a soup called *nsima* (SEE-MA), which the people in his country ate

at every meal, people were
starting to starve.

"My sisters, my parents, they
are all so skinny," William said
sadly. "My father is so hungry
he cannot see. We only eat
once a day now."

All of their other crops had
also dried up and died, so there
was nothing for his family to
sell to make money.

Since William's family did not have money, he also was not able to go to school. This made him very sad, as he liked studying and learning about new things.

Geoffrey was not able to go to school either. Only Gilbert was able to go to school since his father was the district chief.

"I miss school. I miss learning. I miss eating three meals each day. I am hot," William listed as he held up fingers on his hands. He knew that it was not good to dwell on the trials he was facing, but he was so unhappy, and he knew that Geoffrey would understand how sad he felt. Gilbert also felt sad for his friends. He knew how much William loved to learn and how hard it must be to miss out on school each day.

Without school, William did not have much to do. Without food, he did not have much energy. So he sat under the mango tree, day after hot day.

CHAPTER 2
The Library

After a few weeks, William
grew tired of sitting under the
mango tree. He did not want
to be hot and bored. He did not
want to feel sad. He did not
want to waste away.

"If I cannot feed my body,

I will find a way to feed my mind," he said softly.

"I will go down the road to the library," William said out loud.

William walked into the small library. The librarian, Ms. Edith Sikelo, greeted him.

"Have you come to read some books?" she asked with a smile. William nodded, feeling a little bit shy.

"Here is how this is done," Ms. Sikelo said with a soft smile. "Here are all of the books," she said, waving her hands.

"And this is where you fill out a card if you want to take a book home to read." Ms. Sikelo handed him a card. William took a deep breath and then smiled. The smell of the books made him happy.

He did not know that the

library would have books about everything he could think of! William grabbed a few books and sat down on the floor. He started to read, and before he knew it, hours had passed by.

On his next visit to the library, William wanted to find books on science. He had a hard time reading English, but William worked hard to read the words in the books by using a dictionary and looking at the pictures.

When school let out, William took Gilbert to the library with him to find more science books. In the first book William

21

spotted, he found the answer to a question he had asked for years. William had always wanted to know how part of his country got electricity. All he knew was that the Shire River flowed downhill until it reached a power plant. This book showed him that the water turned a huge wheel called a turbine, and that turbine made electricity.

"Look, Gilbert! The big wheel is moved by the water, and then it makes our lights work!" William said in a loud voice.

The boys smiled at one another. It was fun to learn about so many new things! They liked to learn about what made things work. When they were younger, they used to take apart radios and learn how to put them back together. Sometimes they would fix them for people if the radios were broken. Learning about power had always been fun for them.

William kept going to the library and reading all of the books he could. He learned about engines, radios, and farming. He learned more about electricity. But what he was most excited to learn about was something that looked like the pinwheels he used to make as a child, only much, much larger. William learned about windmills.

Windmills

Windmills can produce electricity and pump water.

"Windmills can produce electricity and pump water," William read out loud. He checked his dictionary, which sat next to the library book, to make sure he understood the words.

William leaned back in his chair and stared at the windmill in the book. He closed his eyes and began to think about how electricity and water would help his family.

"I will build a windmill," William said to Gilbert. "A windmill can bring electricity. Electricity is a way to pump water. I will save my family."

William had fed his mind well. He was no longer hot and bored. William had an idea. That day, he left the library with a big smile.

CHAPTER 3

The Junkyard

William left the library and ran down the road.

"Where are you running?" people in the village called out. "It is too hot to run!"

"What are you doing?" they asked when William ran to

the junkyard and began pulling

items into a pile.

"Yes!" William cried out as he found items he could use. Some pipes, bolts, and even a tractor fan all made their way from the junkyard to William's home.

"Why is that boy playing with trash?" the people in the village asked one another. "Has he gone mad?"

After William had gone to the junkyard for many days, William's father grew worried.

"What are you doing, Son?" he asked.

"I have a plan," William said. "Please, Father, let me work."

William's sisters grew angry at the mess that he made. "William will not let us clean his room!"

"What is the matter with our son?" William's mother asked. "Other boys do not behave this way," she said with a frown.

William's father smiled. "The
boy has a plan. Let us see what
he can do."

For several weeks, William
made trips to and from the
junkyard. He found copper

wire, bottle caps, more pipes,
and even a broken bike with a
headlight. Near the back of the
kitchen, in the shade of a large
tree, William sat down in the
dirt with all of his items, and

he made some tools.

"This is a perfect spot for the wind. I can make a great windmill out of this for sure," he said to the wind, for no one else was around. "I will make electric wind!"

Gilbert stopped by as William worked.

"William, how is it going?" he asked.

"I am missing a few parts, I

think. I do not have any money to buy them," William said, looking around.

"I can help," Gilbert said.

William and Gilbert went in search of the last parts for

the windmill. Gilbert used the last bit of money he had.

"You are the greatest friend I ever had," William said to him. "Thank you!"

CHAPTER 4
The Windmill

For many days William worked on his windmill.

Bang! went his tools against the metal.

"Squawk!" went the village chickens as they ran from the loud noises.

"What is that boy doing now?" said the villagers as they walked past.

"Oof!" William said as he dropped a heavy pipe.

"Can we help you make electric wind?" asked Gilbert, looking at the windmill that William had put together. William smiled at the kind offer of help. His friends were just who he needed then.

"Yes! Grab your *pangas*. Let's go to the forest," he said as they held up the windmill blades.

The boys found some blue gum trees. They cut down some of the small trees, then hammered them together and made a tall wooden tower.

William climbed to the top of the tower and looked down. It felt high enough.

"This is good," he said to himself.

"Get some rest, boys!" he said as the sun went down. "Tomorrow is the day!"

The next morning Geoffrey and Gilbert were at the tower before William got out of bed.

"Come on, hurry up," they teased him when he came outside. William and Geoffrey worked on a way to get the

blades onto the tower. They
used a rope as a pulley. It
looked like it would work!

William smiled and climbed the tower.

"Bring it up!" he shouted to Geoffrey and Gilbert. The two boys heaved the windmill into the air.

"Oof, this is heavy!" Gilbert said, panting.

"And it is big!" Geoffrey added, his arms shaking a bit.

Finally, it was high enough. Geoffrey climbed the tower

to William, and the boys got to work placing the fan on the wooden tower.

By this time, many villagers had crowded around. They looked up at this strange tower.

"The boy has gone mad," they said to one another. "What is this mess?"

The villagers stared, some pointed and laughed, and others just shook their heads.

CHAPTER 5
The Light Bulb

William and Geoffrey climbed down the tower. Then William ran into his room. He came back outside with a light bulb and a long copper wire wrapped around a reed. He climbed the tower again.

"What is he doing now?" the villagers asked. From up on the tower, William could see his family at the back of the crowd. They looked scared for him.

He knew that people thought he had gone mad, but he did not care. William's hands shook, but he hung on to the tower quietly, and he waited for the wind.

For a bit, it felt like there was no wind. Then it started—just a light breeze at first, and then a gust that shook the tower.

"Whoa!" thought William, as the tower swayed back and forth a bit.

"Oh!" gasped the crowd below.

"The boy is going to fall!" cried one woman. But William held on.

The windmill blades began to

turn with the wind. The wind kept blowing, and the blades spun faster. Holding on to the tower with his legs, William held the light bulb fast in his hands.

There was a small flicker of light. The crowd gasped.

"Did you see that?" one man shouted.

Everyone stared at William. William held his breath. The light bulb suddenly burned

bright, like the hot sun.

"Yes!" William cried. "I have
made electric wind!"

"He did it!" cried a man from the village.

"Well done, boy!" cried another.

William's father cheered as he grabbed William's mother and swung her around.

The villagers all clapped and yelled for William. He had done it! Electric wind!

When the bulb started to burn his hands, William climbed

down from the tower. He looked around at the smiling faces and then again to his windmill.

"I am only just starting," he said. "I will go even bigger. One day my windmills will bring all of us light and water."

CHAPTER 6

Dreams

In the years after making his first windmill, William was able to bring light to his home. He learned about better and safer ways to use the windmill and how to use solar power to pump water.

William was always learning
and trying new things.
Sometimes his ideas did not
work, but he kept trying.

One day a teacher from the
school came to William.

"William, will you start a
science club at the school? The
students look up to you and
want to learn from you," he
said.

William was happy to teach

the students at the school! He made them a windmill so that they could power a radio and listen to music and the news. He told them about science.

"So many things around you can be used again," he told the students. "In science we can invent and create. We can change our world and make things better."

Moving Windmills

The story of William Kamkwamba does not stop here. After word spread of his windmill, William went on to travel to America and talk about science. His statement "I try, and I made it" spoke

to the hearts of many people.
When he went back to Africa,
he found out that he would
be able to go to school again.
William went to the African
Leadership Academy and
graduated, making his parents
very proud. He also worked
with his friend Bryan and
wrote a book about his own life.
After this, he went on to study
at Dartmouth College in New

Hampshire, United States, and graduated in 2014.

William wanted to find a way to help families in Malawi. In 2008, he helped create Moving Windmills Project, which was created to help people learn about farming and to solve hard problems that people face in their lives.

Moving Windmills Project has helped build wells, installed solar power to homes and businesses, updated schools, and provided new books for local schools and libraries.

William's love of learning and his desire to learn and grow will continue to reach people young and old and make their lives better.

"I try, and I made it!"
–William Kamkwamba

MORE BOOKS FROM
THE GOOD AND THE BEAUTIFUL LIBRARY

Brave Little Ruby
by Shannen Yauger

Helen Keller—Into the Light
by Shannen Yauger

GOODANDBEAUTIFUL.COM